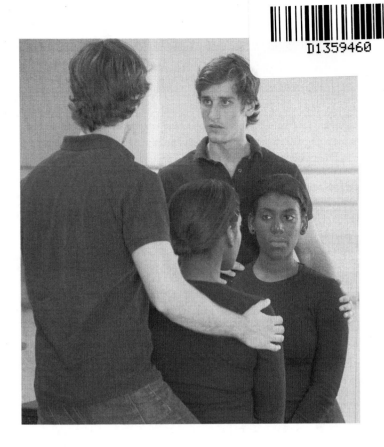

THE ACTOR'S LANDSCAPE
a pocket book of explorations and exercises for the actor

by Cynthia Henderson
Second Edition

Gateways Books & Tapes
Nevada City, California

For Justin whose own self exploration is a constant reminder to me of how beautifully intricate the Being is. Thank you.

THE ACTOR'S LANDSCAPE

Text Copyright © 2009 by Cynthia Henderson

Photos © 2009 by Cynthia Henderson

Cover photos by Sheryl Sinkow

Cover design by Marvette Kort

Some material in this book has appeared in its present form or in earlier textual versions in the following publication:

Understanding Character Through Self, Editions Sherpa, 2004

All Rights Reserved, Printed in the USA, First Printing

ISBN: 978-0-89556-121-3

Published by Gateways Books & Tapes

IDHHB, Inc., PO Box 370, Nevada City, CA 95959 USA

(800) 869-0658 or (530) 271-2239, FAX: (530) 272-0184

Library of Congress – CIP data applied for

CONTENTS

Don't distrust your own innate abilities.

—Lloyd Richards

THE ACTOR'S LANDSCAPE

a pocket book of explorations and exercises for the actor

FOREWORD

As actors we are responsible for making choices that actively pursue the objectives of our characters. In making these dramatic choices, we also inherently choose to expose our true nature, our most basic self. To an actor, or anyone for that matter, this can be terrifying. The actor may start to judge his or herself and worry about what the other group members are thinking of them. This way of thinking inhibits the actor's work and therefore trust becomes very important. The key to achieving the level of openness needed to make effective choices lies in trust, primarily trust in oneself.

As actors, we cannot be successful without allowing ourselves to fail first in order to succeed. We learn more from our mistakes than our victories. In class, Cynthia often quoted Ms. Frizzle, the eccentric elementary school teacher, from the children's book series *The Magic School Bus*. Cynthia's class would not have been complete unless she said, "Take chances, make mistakes, and get messy!"

This idea of trust was immensely important for us when considering the impulses that we had when working with partners within a scene. These impulses represent our "child-like mentality" attempting to come out to play. A child never second guesses him- or herself. Children just do. This is precisely what Cynthia's book encourages. It also encourages the actor to enjoy the journey that he or she will take without worrying about the results.

Foreword contributions from students: Gary Howell, Joanna Krupnick, Max Lawrence, Bryan Plofsky, Jay Schmidt, Lauren Wightman

A THOUGHT

I have been a student, professional performer and teacher of acting. Throughout my career I have worked with the ideas of great people ranging from Stanislavski, Goethe, Uta Hagen and Sanford Meisner to the philosophies of Taoism and other metaphysical teachings. There are countless methods, approaches, new teachers bringing forward new schools of thought and many of those ideas have reinvigorated acting in one way or another. However, one thing I've noticed is that no matter how inspiring the concept, how eye opening the exercise, someone else had done it before at some point. The idea of a "groundbreaking" or "new" concept is often little more than modifications of past great ideas, suited to the needs of the individual actor. This by no means is meant to detract from the great minds who have served as inspirations to all of us. I suppose I point this out to keep myself in check as I realize, "Wow, I just had a great idea." The idea may be great but it may not always be new. The concepts and exercises that I am going to share with you come from a variety of great minds that have inspired me to try things out until they work.

THE ACTOR'S LANDSCAPE

I have a theory. I am not a psychologist, keep this in mind. I minored in psychology as an undergraduate student, which is just enough knowledge to get me in trouble. My theory developed largely from a possible misunderstanding within the scientific community of a quote by psychologist William James who wrote in 1908: "We are making use of only a small part of our possible mental and physical resources" (*The Energies of Men*). From there arose a popular scientific rumor that states we humans use only ten percent of our brains consciously. I hypothesize that we may use only five percent of what I like to call our Psychological and Emotional (or Actor's) Landscape *consciously*. In his studies of human development Carl Jung discovered that humans have a "preconscious psychic disposition that enables a [person] to react in a human manner." Looking at this statement from the viewpoint of his discussions on *Archetypal Patterns,* there are an infinite variety of emotions which point back to these patterns. Since these potential emotional capabilities tend not to be under our conscious control, we often fear them and deny their existence through some form of repression.

The Actor's Landscape theory works on the belief that we are born with an intensely passionate and vast emotional range which frankly makes us capable of anything. It is through social conditioning that our neural pathways reposition themselves on certain cognitive developmental levels in order to channel these emotions and tendencies into less harmful and more socially acceptable behaviors. However, beneath this fine layer of social conditioning lurk some exciting as well as frightening aspects of the human psyche. We are capable of giving the most profound and unconditional love as well being capable of the most hideous crimes known to mankind. These extremes are parts of the human makeup, just as all the variations in between are. Arguably it is due to societal dictates such as "civilized people don't do this," "little girls do that," "big boys don't cry," and so on, that we exist for the most part in a state of emotional indigestion. That statement is not an advocacy for total anarchy; but in its zeal to create a civilized community, our society has also squelched some important aspects of who we are. I have informally observed that by the time many children reach the age of approximately seven, they are fairly close to sitting on many important impulses. As actors it is necessary for us to get back in touch with both the fun and the sometimes dangerous aspects of who we are, at the core of our ability to be. When you have to play a character like Hitler it is important to understand the part of yourself that is capable of mass murder on a scale that would, and did, horrify the world community. Would you act upon such impulses in your own life? One would hope not – but understanding that you are capable of this type of behavior as well as looking into why someone would do such a thing is extremely important to the actor's work. The same holds true for playing a heroic figure like Joan of Arc. It is equally important to know and understand that her kind of faith, courage, and devotion to something so much larger and important than the self, is already within you. These are among the discoveries that are so important to the work of an actor.

The Actor's Landscape Theory has other aspects to it. Once the actor accepts that these traits are locked away within and not being used, he or she must find a way to access them. It's a process of relearning something already known, but long forgotten. I believe that for the most part I am not teaching my students something that they don't already know how to do. As a civilized species we've simply forgotten how to access these aspects of self. Unfortunately, because a synapse fired wrong, the social conditioning was unhealthy, or a person is wired toward certain tendencies, there are people in society who know all too well how to live in one or the other of the two extremes with no middle ground to act as a balance. Our job as actors is to be aware of this very lethal trap and find ways to explore the Actors Landscape in order to enrich a character's life and then very deftly step away when the curtain comes down on the performance. It's an interesting theory that I have been exploring for a few years now. I'm still working out the kinks and very likely will continue to do so until I'm returned to the earth from whence I came. The following exercises are but a few of many that I use; these, however, are some I've found to be most helpful to the actors I've worked with, in discovering the depths of their Actor's Landscape.

PART ONE: A STARTING POINT

SAFE SPACE

Before any honest work can begin in the studio, there needs to be an understanding that everything that happens or is said in the studio does not become hallway gossip. This is the first step in the creation of *safe space* as I work with it. Safe space is often an unspoken understanding among actors as they begin the process of working in a class or on a production. Unfortunately some folks don't always "get the memo," and the work sometimes suffers for the backstage or hallway talk. When walking into the studio it would always be a good idea to keep in mind the "four virtues" of theatre as outlined in a wonderful book titled *A Practical Handbook for the Actor* by Melissa Bruder et al. The virtues outlined in the book are humility: understanding that you can be wrong; generosity: acknowledging when others are on the right track; consideration: respecting the process of other actors without interference; and tact: knowing when and to whom to voice your opinions. As the actor's work, by nature, is highly personal and often subjective, keeping the theatre clear of unnecessary "drama" is desirable for all involved in the creative process.

If something happens in the studio which is harmful to the process then, by all means, find an appropriate time and place to speak with the Director or Instructor. If you don't agree with the way another actor is working, look at it from that actor's point of view; he or she may not agree with the way you work. Never take it upon yourself to teach or direct your colleagues. It is often viewed as an invasion of privacy or process and is rarely, if ever, appreciated. If the other actor's process is hindering your own, then speak to the Stage Manager or Instructor – it is their job to redirect if necessary. This keeps the space open to evolution and provides the actor with a safety net on which to fall and to be propelled back up and in a more useful direction. These are the basics of creating and nurturing the safe space, so that the actor can get on with the business of finding the truth within for the development of character.

WHAT IS ACTING?

acting ('æk tɪŋ) – Pronunciation (ak-ting)

–adjective

1. serving temporarily, esp. as a substitute during another's absence; not permanent; temporary: the acting mayor.

2. designed, adapted, or suitable for stage performance.

3. provided with detailed stage directions for the performer: an acting version of a play.

–noun

4. the art, profession, or activity of those who perform in stage plays, motion pictures, etc.

During our initial meeting as a class, the first thing I often do is ask students what springs to mind when they hear the word *acting*. The students' answers range through "pretending," "living," "finding the truth no matter what" and so on. We end up working our chalk board full of ideas down to a very simple sentence. Acting is living truthfully in the given circumstances. How do we go about finding these truths? How do we allow ourselves to believe in the character's circumstances in order to live these truths? This is where the idea of understanding more about yourself as a human being in order to understand your character comes into play. I spend a lot of time allowing students (and myself when I am working on a character for a show) a space to ask themselves why a character would do this or allow that. Then I put the challenge before them to ask what circumstances it would take for them to allow this or that to happen. Often a fun and exciting dialog begins to occur between the actor and "character" at that moment. How do we get to the point where such a dialog can occur? This is where training and ways of rehearsing come into play. Some exercises require a group, but most are exercises and meditations that can be done on your own.

BREAKING THE ICE TO TRUST

BE AS A CHILD

"Be as a child," that sounds almost biblical. A biblical parable is where I first encountered this idea that adults should take time out to look at life from the perspective of a child. In Matthew 18:3 of the *Holy Bible,* it's a lesson Jesus gave to his followers: "I tell you the truth, unless you change and become like little children, you will never enter the kingdom of heaven." In his lesson he primarily focused on the simple faith with which children approach life and belief in him. For the actor it pertains to an honest faith and belief in one's abilities to work believably. Have you ever observed young children playing? It doesn't matter what they are playing or where they are, because in that moment of time, they are who they say they are. Children quite simply assign the role – "I'm the mommy, you're the daddy and you're the baby"; set the location – "This is the house, that's the car"; and the play begins until someone gets tired of being the baby and decides she is a race car driver and takes off for the Indy 500 in the family car. Of course the job of the actor is more complex; but at its core, it is not that much different from simply believing in your character and circumstances with the easy faith of a child.

On occasion I will have an acting class take a day to observe a child. Since most of them are childless, I suggest that they do some babysitting, keep an eye on a younger sibling or a relative's young child. Watch the child at play either alone or with a group of other children. When young children play, so important is each moment, that they shut out everything else. They erect an almost perfect "fourth wall." The fourth wall, short definition, is an imaginary wall which allows an actor to live the character's life without acknowledging the presence of the audience. For the actor, the challenge is to allow yourself to jump into the life of your character with the abandonment and joyful relish of a child, while maintaining the integrity of the playwright's intentions.

TANGLED

This can be a useful and fun "ice breaker" method of introducing a new class or young cast to one another. A group of six or more link hands in a haphazard fashion across the center of a tight circle they've formed and attempt to unravel to form an open circle. The only major rule in this exercise is that the actors should keep their hands clasped as they work to disentangle. The exercise itself is simple. It is the process that the individuals go through to get into the open circle which is most useful to the formation of an ensemble.

The newly introduced group begins the process of communication. They talk, instruct, and listen to one another. Oftentimes this is accompanied by a great deal of laughter mixed with frustration. They discover, without much intellectualizing, some initial strengths and weaknesses within the group and work to augment or compensate. It is also often the first intimate physical contact they have with one another. Later they recall that hands, feet, heads, backs, and pelvises were in contact with people they had, in many cases, just met and they didn't think anything of it. The foundation of open communication and profess-ional trust between actors can begin.

ELEVATE

One actor should lie with his back on the floor. The ensemble gathers around the actor. Each member of the ensemble must have at least one hand touching the actor on the floor. The entire ensemble then lifts the actor off the floor and holds him up at shoulder height. When it is right to do so, the ensemble gently places the actor back onto the floor. The actor will then switch places with another actor, until every member of the ensemble has had the experience. Please always be aware of safety when lifting or being lifted.

The variation on this game that makes it an exercise is simple. After the first few times, no verbal communication should be allowed. To add a degree of playfulness I will occasionally take my class through a story that they act out during the exercise. The story goes that they are all cave people and a sickness has swept across the valley. The medicine woman (I call her Uuraah) knows of a tree which gives life to those stricken with the illness. However, in order for the tree's powers to work, the entire clan must carry the stricken individual to the tree for healing. Communication is without language, only sounds, and the process goes on until every member of the clan (including Uuraah) has been carried and healed. Upon completion it can be an interesting process for the ensemble to sit and discuss how the experience affected each of them.

LIVING SCULPTURES

Part of this exercise came out of a game of "Red Light, Green Light." In it the participants are at one end of the space and the leader is at the other end. The leader counts as fast as he or she can to ten and shouts "Red Light!" The participants all run to touch the leader before the shout of "red light." Once "red light" is called, all must freeze right where they are until the call of "green light" and the ten count begins again. The sculptures part of the exercise comes from the idea of not being so literal in our interpretations of stimulus and need.

The exercise can have two variations. One variation is as a group exercise where everyone works as an individual. In this form it is more like the "Red Light, Green Light" game. The ensemble begins by simply moving about the space at a moderate walking pace. They weave in and out between one another without colliding, being aware of who and what is around them at all times. It is useful for the actors to work on spatial awareness. It's sometimes helpful when time constraints are an issue to combine two or more lessons into one. The group leader then instructs the ensemble to pick up the pace, while maintaining an awareness of their surroundings. As the ensemble picks up their pace the leader calls out a word. The word should be something

simple which encourages a visceral response from the actor. Words such as *storm, flower, child, razor, birth, death* are useful. When the word is called out, the leader claps her hands sharply as a signal to freeze (red light) and the ensemble should immediately freeze into a shape which gives a sense of how the word affects each of them. Their minds should be on their surroundings in the given moment and not on what word is coming next. Let the ensemble hold the shape for a few moments in order for the meaning of their shape to sink in and then call for them to begin walking the space once again (green light). This can continue as long as the group needs.

The second variation of this exercise is a bit more complicated, as it involves partnering. The partners do not get a chance to discuss the words that will be called. Actually in both variations of this exercise the ensemble should never know what the leader is going to call.

The second variation of Living Sculptures begins with the partners doing the Mirror Exercise. In the Mirror Exercise the idea is to mirror the movements of the person in front of you. The movements should be smooth and seamless.

The exercise is not meant to trick the partner into not getting a move correctly. This is an exercise whose purpose is to form a connection between the partners. It's an exchange of energy that over time can become tangible enough that physically looking directly at the other actor is not wholly necessary in order to pick up on a person's state of being. The ensemble should be encouraged to make use of the entire body during this exercise. As the Mirror Exercise is being done, the leader again calls out a word and signals a freeze. The softer chime of a bell is sometimes preferable for this variation, so as not to shock the partners out of the connection they've formed. In the first variation, there are generally a lot of sounds and thoughts to cut through so a clap is more useful.

After the call, partners should react as one and freeze into a shape that uses the two of them to convey how the word affects both as one. A stipulation that also comes with partnering is that they should at this moment make physical contact so that the shape (or sculpture) is one shared reaction to the stimulus. Allow the partners to hold the shape for a moment and then call for them to end physical contact and resume the mirror exercise from where they are.

The actors should not go back to neutral. This allows them to continue within the moment. It is never useful to go back to a previous moment. You will find that living from one moment to the next is a cornerstone to all the exercises in this book. As with the previous variation, this exercise can go as long as necessary to the work of the ensemble.

THIS IS BLISS

This is a variation on the trust exercise in which an individual falls back into the arms of another, trusting that he or she will be caught. The Trust Fall exercise may have developed as a form of group psychotherapy and has since become a basic part of team building. In the 1960s Julian Beck and Judith Malina of *The Living Theatre* used the *exercise* of having audience members leap from the stage to be caught by 6 to 8 actors from the troupe. A friend of mine who witnessed this found the experience to be *beyond* astounding. A contemporary variation of this exercise would be *crowd surfing* which became widely popular during the 1990s at grunge concerts. When I started using this exercise for an acting class, I thought it would be useful in building the sense of ensemble if I had them work as a group. The ensemble forms a tight circle and one member stands in the center. The individual closes his eyes, holds both feet together, allowing the arms to hang loosely at the sides, and without attempting to catch oneself, says "this is bliss" then falls back into the ensemble. The ensemble's job is to catch the person and slowly hand him off to the next person until everyone has "supported the weight of responsibility" for their colleague. Each member takes a turn. The other thing that brought the group idea to mind occurred when I re-read my syllabus. I had written, "We will not be afraid to fall down in this class because there will always be someone there to pick us up." I think of it as a physical reminder of the contract we make with one another when classes begin. It also begins the work of trusting self and others that is so necessary to the actors' work.

What do you see?

ON OBSERVATION

Look around you. What do you see? What do
you hear? What do you pick up from the people
around you? Often actors get so caught up in
what's happening to them, to their character, that
they may neglect the needs of others who share
the space with them. Observation exercises are
necessary for the actor to develop a true sense of
not only what's happening to oneself but also
what's happening around oneself and to others. I
often tell my class that even when the show is
centered on your character; it isn't completely
about that character. Basically the need is to get
over yourself long enough to see what's going on
in the world of the play. The most amazing
performances occur not when the actors are
primarily focused on what's important to them; the
amazing performances happen when the focus is
on those things outside of themselves. Ask
yourself what you really see when you walk into

the room. Are you honestly listening to what's being said to you and around you? How do these things affect you? How do your actions affect others? If you have trouble answering these types of questions, it may be a good idea to work on your observational skills.

WHO STARTED?

In this theatre game of observation, the ensemble sits in a circle while one member leaves the space. One person in the group begins a rhythm or movement that the others copy. The member who was outside comes in and stands in the center of the circle and tries to figure out who is starting the movements. The group leader should change the movements subtly on occasion. Once the person at center figures out who is starting the movements, he or she switches with that person, and so on until everyone has taken a turn. The keener the observer is in the exercise, the faster the turnover.

WHAT'S DIFFERENT?

I have been told that this is hands down one of the most fun exercises we do in class. It is also the exercise that many students want to have a photo of, at its conclusion. This is an observation exercise that involves dividing the ensemble into two groups. They then line up, two lines facing one another, paired with whomever they happen to be facing. Give them time to take in every aspect of one another, then have them turn their backs to one another. Have them change three things about their appearance. When they've all completed the changes, have them face one another. The partners are then to point out what is different from before. Have the ensemble turn their backs again, and this time they change five things, then seven, and then nine; see how far you can take the group before they run out of things to change. Besides helping the actor learn to look very closely at the partner, this is a way to ease them into the idea of taking what they come in with as a base and building from there. I find that laughter is useful in helping smooth the way to the inevitable frustrations which will come as the work begins to demand that you look into who you are, with honesty.

ON BEING QUIET: MEDITATION

An important part of learning to observe is the ability to be quiet within. Being quiet is not something that most people would readily associate with an actor; yet it is an essential component of our work. In order to release the various distractions that hinder the actor from focusing on the work at hand, a sense of inner quiet is necessary. The following are some exercises which should assist you in centering so that you can begin focusing on your work and the larger world beyond that work.

TOUCH AN OBJECT

This meditation was passed on to me by a friend, an artist and author, named E.J. Gold. I was introduced to it as a way to release my over dependence on "out-thinking" myself in my daily habits. I quickly realized that it could be very easily applied to the needs of the actor. One of the things we often do as actors is over analyze the character's circumstances to the point that we render the character unplayable. We forget simply to do what needs to be done in order for the character to be able to achieve his or her goals or objectives.

The exercise is a simple one and can be done as a group or alone. You need only to sit quietly and be instructed by a group leader to touch an object. This object can be anything: a rock, a pencil, desk, shoe, and so on. The objective simply is to do what needs to be done while not distracting self with a lot of unnecessary thought. The Taoist concept of "no mind" is what is germane here. Many students upon first encountering this exercise feel that it is almost impossible to do. A student once said that she would find herself feeling sorry for the something she did not touch so would make sure she touched it the next time the instruction of "touch an object" was given. She laughed as she realized that so desperate was she to "figure out the answer" to the simplicity of doing, that she gave life and feeling to a rock, spent most of her time listening for hidden meaning in the instructions, and missed the whole point, initially! That's often what we do as actors. We can't stop thinking long enough to simply do. I find that if I catch my mind wandering for a moment during the course of a rehearsal or performance, it is useful for the character if I "touch an object" in order to re-ground and get on with the business of living the character's life with simplicity and integrity.

The set up for the exercise is simple. Sit quietly with only a candle, two or three objects, and a chime. The chime and candle are optional after you get the hang of the meditation.

In the case of a group there should be one person who guides the meditation. If you are working alone simply place one thought in your mind – "touch an object" – and allow that to be the only thought you have for the next ten minutes. Increase the time as you improve. Light your candle. The candle is to be used as a simple point of refocusing, if you find it necessary. The chime is used as a signal that it is time to clear your mind of all outside distractions and focus on one objective which is simply to "touch an object."

Without giving thought to why, what or how, reach out and touch an object. That sounds simple enough. As you get better at clearing your mind and focusing on the one objective, this exercise can be used to assist in grounding yourself in the character's reality during actual performance work.

CANDLE EXERCISE

This is an exercise that was introduced to me by my son via a physicist and visual artist named Claude Needham. My son, Justin, became interested in all things science and began working with this scientist while we lived in California. Being nine years old, at that time, his attention span was often that of a gnat, but he had an intense interest in what Claude was doing. To help him work on his attention and observation skills Claude had Justin begin working with breaking down the properties of a lit candle. My son would sit for twenty to thirty minutes with this candle. He would observe its flame, checking and logging in a little note book the colors, how the wax dripped, flame rotation, and so on. I noted an amazing thing. My nine year old hurricane of energy began to notice things he'd tended to ignore before. He had always been able to gauge the feelings of others in the space with him, but this ability became more acute. He watched and took in more, his observational skills increased considerably. I talked to Claude about the exercise, and he gave me the basics of what he had Justin do. I took the exercise and adapted it to the needs of an actor.

Like the previous meditation exercise, the set up is simple. You will need a white, unscented tapered candle, a simple but sturdy candle holder, and a small note book to log your observations. Sit quietly in a space where you won't be disturbed for at least fifteen to twenty minutes.

Clear your mind of all distractions and light your candle. Using all of your senses, notice every conceivable and inconceivable thing about the candle. What does the lighting of the candle smell like? How does the wick accept the flame? What colors occur in the flame before it settles into ... how many colors? Ask yourself these and many other questions as you observe the candle's many physical properties. However, the exercise does not end there. After breaking down the natural physical properties and noting them, how does the candle react to various imposed stimuli? How does it react to a slight breeze? If you tip it, does the wax always fall where you think it will, and so on? You then will note how the exercise affects you. Remember to keep all questions about yourself within the context of working with the candle. The exercise is not about you, per se, it is about working with the candle. How it affects you is a by-product of working on something outside of yourself.

As your work with the candle progresses you will apply this same level of attention on your acting partner. Observe all aspects of the person(s) you are working with just as you have been doing with the candle. Note the little idiosyncratic behaviors of your partner, how the person reacts to various stimuli, and so on. You will also note your own reactions to things the partner says and does in reaction to what you have done. As with the candle exercise, keep in mind the work is not about you, it is about your partner first. Don't allow yourself to become analytical while working with this process. Though the work is not directly about you, allow yourself to feel and be affected by what is going on.

THE BEACH

This meditation can take whatever form you need it to. The description I am giving is the one I prefer to use.

The actors are taken through variation one of the Living Sculptures exercise which was described earlier. The leader will determine when the space is ready for the shift into meditation. He or she will then have the actors take the final sculpture and imagine that they are on a frozen landscape. As they hold the, now ice, sculpture, the sun burns brighter, and the ice sculptures melt onto the ground until all actors are on their backs with arms at their sides taking on the image of water puddles. These "puddles" reform into the actors' bodies. The frozen ground gently continues to melt under the sun and reveals grass which wilts under the sun to reveal sand. Take the actors through a series of descriptions of their surroundings that are not so specific as to have everyone see the same things. For example, have them "Listen to the sounds of your beach," "What do you smell?" "Without actually opening your eyes, what do you see?" "What are some of things you feel as you lie on the sand?" "What do you sense around you?" "Something blows across your face." "Watch it." Within the world they create during this meditation, tension is released through droplets of sweat that form on the body and fall off to be absorbed by the sand. Relaxation is aided by allowing for a visualization of light moving slowly down the body from the crown of the head to the toes. As the leader calls off where the light is, the actors are asked to release that area of the body to gravity. The next phase of the meditation involves an appreciation of the physical body for what it is, does, and goes through on a daily basis to support the non-physical being. After this portion, the being is encouraged to drift up from the body to go on a journey over the ocean, leaving the physical body safely on the shore. The journey is flight oriented and the actor is asked to observe "an activity that is happening in water." What that activity is and how close they get to it is entirely up to the actors. The discussion about this section, after the meditation is done, has always been fascinating. To continue; after awhile have the body compel the being to return and reintegrate the two, allowing a moment for the being and body to acknowledge gratitude for one another. Once the being and body are reintegrated, bring the actors back into the studio space.

Once the meditation is complete, it's useful to give the ensemble the opportunity to talk about their individual experiences. If no one brings up the observation that all were given the exact same instructions, but each approached it differently, the leader should bring it up. Besides pointing out centering and making discoveries about how they each approach an experience, it should also be noted that just as each actor approached similar instructions differently, the same can be said of how an actor approaches a character that someone else has done. I bring this up because many beginning actors make the mistake of thinking that they should do a character the way they've seen it done before, by someone else.

A very short exercise called Make Me Laugh has the same goal. Give the simple instruction of "make me laugh." Each actor then has to do something to make the leader laugh. Point out that, for the most part, each individual had his or her own approach to making the same person laugh. The approach is based on one's own psychological and emotional makeup. The same holds true for character work. Though they played the same character, Phylicia Rashad's "Witch" in the Broadway production of Stephen Sondheim's *Into the Woods* was very different from Bernadette Peters' "Witch" in the original Broadway production. The character is the same, but the actors are very different women. This can be seen as the practical point to an otherwise esoteric exercise.

FOCUS AND RELEASE

The release of unnecessary tension (as described in the Beach meditation) is extremely important in this work. You need to be available to give and receive energy as well as note and be affected by your surroundings. This is difficult to accomplish if you are still wondering about the $55 parking ticket you received on the corner of Amsterdam Ave. and 160th St. However, it is also important to know what energy and tension to release and what is necessary to keep for use in your work. Often, actors will shake themselves into a mad frenzy, flinging various appendages haphazardly about until they have no useable energy for the performance. They find themselves all charged up with nothing but unfocused energy. The idea behind "shake outs" and "energy ball" style exercises is to let go of what you don't need, keep what you do need, and know the difference between the two.

ON ENERGY

Energy is something that is often talked about in acting. The giving and receiving of energy to one another and the audience is a key component of the play having a momentum with which to move forward. However, keep in mind that energy means very little if it is not accompanied by an emotional backbone. The emotional backbone allows you to be affected by what's happening and allowing it to come through in everything you do. It is that which gives energy purpose. If an actress were to enter a room and suddenly begin frantically tearing about the room, turning things over, then run out for no apparent reason, the audience would for the most part be quite confused by this sudden burst of random energy which seemed to come from nowhere. However, if the same actress bursts into the room focused on finding her keys with urgency born of a need to be on time for a 9:00 A.M. job interview, the audience can be with her. As she frantically searches and becomes more desperate, her heart races. She checks her watch. She continues searching but cannot find the keys. Her breathing becomes more rapid as she begins to panic. She realizes that she may miss the interview and not get the much-needed job. An organic level of frustration builds, and then she spots the keys. The audience exhales with her relief, and she rushes from the room. She leaves many in the audience hoping she gets the job. This is energy with an emotional backbone. From the moment you walk into the space, it's not about an arbitrary pace you set. The pace is a by-product of how your character's day is going and the effect it has on her. Energy is not an end unto itself; it is the product of a full emotional life.

TRAVELING TREMORS

This is a release exercise. An imaginary ball of energy is passed from person to person through body contact. The ball of energy travels through the body of one person and is then passed on to the next, where it travels the length of that person's body and is passed on, and so forth, until it has passed through the entire ensemble. The purpose is to allow for a focused release and exchange of energy while loosening the body, so the actor is physically available to send and to receive stimuli during the rehearsal or performance.

To assist in achieving the focus necessary, try using the image of a hot potato. To work on shifting energy and intention, change the image as it travels from one actor to another. For instance, start with the hot potato image, but as the actor passes it on to another, change the image to a robin's egg. This allows the energy to keep moving while allowing the actors to shift focus and intention without presupposing how they will work with the energy coming toward them. It keeps the actor present in the moment.

ENERGY PUNCHES

This energy build and exchange exercise has at its foundation the exchange, use, and recycling of the circle of energy that is created between partners. When you stand across from another person you begin the process of an exchange. As a fast way to "pump up" with your partner it definitely has its uses. Stand a safe distance from your partner with arms extended in front of you both. Make sure that your hands do not come into contact with one another. Take time to connect with one another through eye contact. Spot the places on the body that you will be sending energy to. The areas to target for energy placement are the shoulders, the pelvis, and the knees. Without stopping, you then work your way back up; knees, pelvis, shoulders, and finally the forehead. Please don't begin this kind of exercise until both actors acknowledge that they're ready. When both partners are ready, use the breath to ground your energy. Spot each area, then punch and use a martial arts style of "kiai" (pronounced *key-eye*) breath to send energy to each of the target areas beginning with the right fist. Let's look at the word *kiai* for a moment. If the word is broken down into its two parts, you will note that *Ki* means "energy" and *Ai* means "join" or "coming together." Kiai means "joining energy." Kiai is bringing together all possible energy and sending it out on an audible breath. The shout of "kiai" is not actually necessary, but it does assist in focusing the direction of energy expulsion. There are four uses for kiai in martial arts: to startle, to gain attention, to coordinate breathing and muscle contraction, as well as to provide energy. For the

safety check

grounding

final punch stance

end stance

purposes of this exercise, use kiai to coordinate breathing and provide energy for self and partner. The succession should go like this; shoulder, shoulder; hip, hip; knee, knee; then back up with: knee, knee; hip, hip; shoulder, shoulder; forehead. The partners should never make physical contact during this exercise. When punching, do not lean forward at all; that is the reason you make sure you are grounded and ready before beginning. This exercise encourages supported breathing, rapid and purposeful focusing outside of self, as well as the useful exchange of energy. Don't flail, focus.

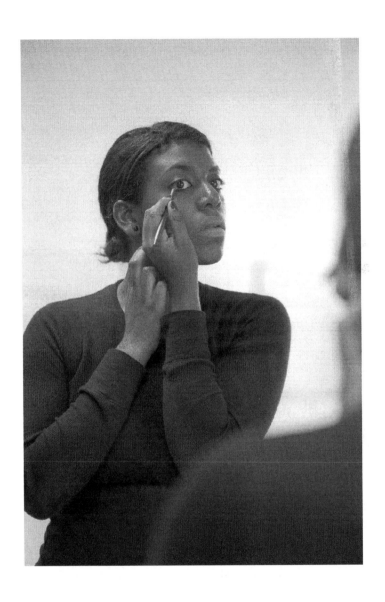

SELF- OBSERVATION

In his book, *Sanford Meisner on Acting*, Meisner introduces his students to the concept of "public solitude." Public Solitude is centered on the idea of living your life as if there is no one watching you. Of course anywhere from 1 to 1,000,000 plus people may be watching you, but live your character's life as if they aren't.

This is a fun exercise which can give actors a great deal of insight into what they are about and how they go about being. The idea came to me, in part, from about thirty seconds of a scene in a movie I watched back in the 1980s. The movie was not that great, but the thirty seconds of the scene stuck with me.

As with many of the exercises in this book, actors can become uncomfortable with what they are faced with when they look "in the mirror"; this is a natural part of our art. You don't have always to be comfortable with whom you are, just being aware and dealing accordingly is all that is necessary.

Take a typical day in your life, any moment within that day will do. At one point during your day take a moment to observe every nuance of what you are doing. It does not matter what you happen to be doing. You can be preparing a meal, brushing your teeth, putting on make up, shaving, taking a shower, changing a baby's diaper, cleaning your contacts, clipping your nails, changing for bed, rehearsal, class, this list can go on indefinitely, but you get the point. Observe what hand you use to do what and how much energy you expend. How does the activity affect you? If you find yourself sorting through old photographs of a loved one who died awhile back, your reaction to the activity is going to be very different than if you were sorting through those same photographs in order to put a surprise collage together for that person as a birthday gift. Be honest with yourself so that you will be honest for us. As you pay close attention to behaviors and habits, don't change them to suit an aesthetic, continue to live the moment. Always pay attention to what you are doing and how you are doing it. It would be advisable to avoid activities such as reading, waking up, or sleeping. These types of passive activities are not useful to the work at hand. When the ensemble meets, each member must recreate the activity in front of the group as if he or she were completely alone. The trap in this exercise is to *perform* the moment and activity. This is why it is so important to be honest and to live the moment with simplicity and integrity.

PERSONAL OBJECTS

This tends to be one of the first assignments I give my acting classes. I will discuss two variations on the same exercise to illustrate how it can be used to introduce the beginning actor to the work at hand as well as to assist the seasoned actor in discovering the things that are important to a character he or she must work with.

The actors are assigned to go home which for actors tends to be wherever they have their possessions in a given moment. They are to give careful consideration to something that means a great deal to them. This object should be tangible, but that is not mandatory. Upon discovering this object they should develop a brief version of the true story which surrounds the object and its meaning in their life. The story must be true in order to allow their fellow actors a full understanding of how important this object is.

The story should be no longer than two minutes and no shorter than one. You may already have an idea of where this exercise is going. It is important that everyone understand what you are attempting to say about this object. The object can be anything. It can be a song, a poem, a stuffed animal, a pet, or a shirt. A student once brought in his parent. The parent was fun because she came in with a personal object of her own, for which the young actor was completely unprepared. When the ensemble meets, each member then presents the personal object to the group. Please remember, this sharing is not a performance. Keep in mind that, as always, this presentation is not about you, it is about the necessity for the group truly to understand why this object is so incredibly special. Approaching this exercise with "well this isn't that important but..." is *not* appropriate. Work to affect your peers and to uplift this special moment that *this* came into your life. Work for something more important than you, and notice how you are affected by this work effort. You may find that it will be the most effective monologue you have delivered to date.

In the second variation of the Personal Objects exercise, you take the same principles of variation one and apply them to your character. Yes, Virginia, your character, upon close inspection, has a "thing of great importance" as well. The twist here is to bring it to the group in character (if it is a class). If you are in a rehearsal process, just simply knowing what that personal special thing is for your character, is a lovely little secret for you to carry throughout the performance. Understand that, like you, your character is in constant evolution, and things can and will change. So, don't feel the need to stick with an object once you discover it during the first week of rehearsals; you have at least four weeks of performances to make new discoveries and if the show has a long run, chances are discoveries made in the first week will be obsolete by the fifth month. Be flexible, be honest, and enjoy your discoveries.

LETTERS

This exploration is a very useful tool for allowing actors to touch base with the depths they need to reach within their characters' life experiences, through their own. This exercise can help move into monologue work rather gracefully. By asking the actors to approach themselves fearlessly; the transition to allowing the character to feel at that depth, in scene work as well as monologue work, can become a less jarring request.

I generally give students a week to think about this exercise. We tend to begin this phase of work during the time that we are exploring the concepts of "as if," "truth of circumstance" and when character analysis is being introduced. It is also the precursor to scripted monologue work for some classes. The actors are asked to think about someone who has affected their lives profoundly, either in a positive or negative way. It must be an honest moment in the actor's life, but one they don't mind having others know about. [I should explain that by this time in the work we have established a "safe space" with the group. It has been agreed that what is said in the space does not leave the space, unless there is a danger to self or others.] The actor is then to write a letter to this person. In the letter the actor is allowed to say something that he or she has always wanted to say but never managed to. The reasons for not saying vary, from the person being written to having died to the actor simply being afraid to say anything. After the letter is written the actor must then edit out all unnecessary lines so that the letter consists of what we call the "heart of the matter." We then work with the letter as one would a monologue. The actors know the person the letter is about extremely well and doesn't have to guess about reactions to what is being said. They know how this person looks, smells, the color of his or her eyes, the sound of his or her laughter, how he or she sounds when they are yelling, and so on. The actors know from experience when to back off and when to push a point because they know this person and how this person affects them. They know everything that they need to know in order honestly to pursue the objective. As they work this "monologue," they begin to experience the level of importance with which to approach the life of a character. The actor also begins to understand viscerally the types of questions one needs to ask as one begins working on the objective and needs of a character. Who the people in the character's life are takes on new and more urgent meaning.

As a delightful by-product, the actor also gains a slight understanding of how important it is to remain true to the finished work written by a playwright. It plants the seed of respect for the words as they are written. You should understand that when I speak of respecting the playwright's work, I am speaking of the finished product. In a workshop situation, the playwright is often in search of ideas that will make his or her work complete. Since part of our job as actors is to respect the words written by finding the truth within them as they are written, if there is time I will occasionally have the actors exchange their "letter monologues." This allows each to memorize and find his or her own truth in words written by a colleague. In turn each actor must listen to someone else's take on a very personal moment in that person's life. It is important to note that when you are writing the letter do not try to work with an event that is still emotionally raw. If the event is still new and raw it is often unplayable.

Give yourself enough distance so that the work can be done, but use something which still has an effect on you. What began as a very simple sounding assignment usually turns out to be more work than many of the students expect. There is a great deal of laughter, often a few tears shed, and some anger expressed during this phase of work. As with all exercises and explorations, this exercise will continue to evolve as my own understanding of the work continues to grow and develop.

PART TWO: PARTNERING

GUIDE AND VOYAGER

There is a book I have read many times entitled *American Book of the Dead (ABD)*, by E.J. Gold, which has inspired many lively discussions in my class. You may wonder what a book on the subject of death and dying has to do with acting; quite a bit actually. When you think about the actor as a potential "Guide" and the audience as the "Voyager" you have the makings of a journey through a labyrinth which separates "life" and "death." How does this work? I ask that you understand that this is an oversimplification of a person's work, which took years of exhaustive research. An important aspect of the *ABD* is that there is a relationship which is very important between the Guide, also known as the reader (the person serving as guide to the dying individual) and the Voyager (the individual who is dying).

Part of this relationship is the responsibility that the Guide has for the Voyager's journey through the labyrinth toward the Sun Absolute (heaven, if you will). This responsibility means that the Guide (in our case the actor) cannot "fall asleep at the wheel." If he or she does, then the Voyager (audience or even the partnering actor) cannot complete this all-important journey they've set out on. Between two or more actors the same principal holds true, except the role of Guide and Voyager change according to the needs of the play. The actors have a unique responsibility to the audience as well as one another to stay awake, alert, and attentive to needs outside of their own. Lest we let voyagers off the hook too easily, they also have a responsibility to the guide. The voyager must develop the ability to trust; to trust the guide's integrity and to trust that, as the voyager, one will be available to receiving and giving energy from and for the guide. I over-simplify, but I think you get the point.

The exercise that brings this, quite heady, concept to life is a simple "blind walk." The actors partner up and one is blindfolded, much like a dying individual who finds himself or herself lost in a labyrinth of friendly and unfriendly guides. In the basic "blind walk" the "sighted" actor takes the blindfolded actor on a walk. However, what I like to do is have the two actors on opposite ends of our work space. A variety of obstacles are then placed between the partners. These obstacles always include physical objects and, for more advanced classes, I also add other distractions that could take the voyager off course. Something as simple as two other actors having an intense discussion could be a distraction. The Voyager must be able to focus on what is important in the moment and follow the Guide's voice. It is the Guide's responsibility to bring the Voyager safely, without as much as a bumped knee, across the space. The partners should not come into physical contact during the exercise. The Guide must get the point across through the use of clear and focused intention. An intention is that thing you *need* for (or from) the other actor. The successful relating of that intention has its test in the other person. For instance, if you are down the hallway and see a child about to touch the blades of a fan in motion, you must be capable of stopping that child *before* you reach him physically. The same necessity for focused intention is true in acting. The Guide's job is to keep the Voyager calm and focused while navigating that voyager through the maze of obstacles. The exercise demands a great deal of focused attention from both actors. Neither can allow himself to be distracted from the needs of the partner.

"I NEED THAT"

I've had first year students ask me on occasion, "When do we get to do a *real* scene?" My answer is always, "When you can communicate effectively without being overly dependent on the words to get you through a scene." "I Need That" is an improvisational scene which gives you only two lines in order to obtain your objective. As in all improvisational scene work, the actors are given, or develop, a situation. They must also have a relationship, history, previous conflict due to the simple fact that theatre is not about the day that nothing happens. One actor is "in" and the other is "out," though not necessarily literally. The actor who is initially "out" needs something, and all the actor is allowed to say is "I need that." The actor who is, initially, "in" has something the other actor needs and is only allowed to say, "I can't give it to you." Even if the circumstances change during the course of the scene, they are only allowed those two lines. Please note that the lines are not interchangeable. Why is this? It is about intention. It is not what you say or even how you modulate your tone to say it. If you focus too much on how you say something you may find yourself giving line readings. Line readings are those moments when the actor steps out of the character's life and attempts to control the scene using an inorganically varied tone of voice in speaking the lines to give a specific direction to another actor. Allow the exercise to be about your behavior, your ability to read your scene partner and respond to what you honestly receive in return. It is about acting on your impulses because you don't have a brilliant playwright giving you all the right things to say. It is about listening with more than your ears. Listen with your entire being. It is about being able to communicate, "I am trying to keep you from making the same mistake again" while saying the line "I can't give it to you." Until you can trust yourself to give over to the work without the need to control it, you truly should not yet attempt works written by the likes of August Wilson, Tennessee Williams, Suzan Lori-Parks, Arthur Miller, Shaw or Shakespeare. That may sound a bit elitist, but truly it isn't. I have a deep respect for the finished works of playwrights and think that we should work to understand how to get our points across so that the eventual partnering of finished script and actor is a work of art.

SLEEP AND STEAL

This improvisational exercise comes from an acting teacher who was extremely influential in my early development as an actor. I have used it for almost every acting class I've worked with and it remains a favorite as well as the moment many of my students remark, "Oh I think I get what you've been talking about." They may not always truly "get it," but the seed has, generally, been planted so that they may later truly understand the aspects that are inherent in the exercise.

The actors are partnered and given the assignment to come up with a relationship that is probable which must include the history between the characters. They need a tangible object that is significant to both partners. The object should be something that is not easily obtained elsewhere. They should have a likely location for one to be asleep. The time of day is important; you are a very different person at 3:00 P.M. than you are at 3:00 A. M. The actors develop the circumstance which serves as the reason the object must be stolen as opposed to asked for. As in the previous exercise who is, literally, "in" and who is "out," initially is important. After everything has been established the character who is "in" takes a nap. This is more difficult than it sounds. The sleeper should not feign sleep but allow the body to fall into a state of rest. One of the "sleeper's" jobs is not to wake up for any reason other than an honest response to something that happens in a given moment. I ask students to avoid "actor knowledge." This means that, of course, the actor is well aware that another actor is in the space. Like many actors, the temptation to "get up and have a scene" can be overwhelming. The actor's job is not to give in to this temptation. The actor may know what's going on but the character doesn't. The sleeper should only wake when something happens to *make* him do so. The concept of not doing anything unless a stimulus makes an action necessary is the basis of Stanislavski's rule of "acting is reacting." The actor "stealing" should focus on both the objective at hand and how her actions are affecting the "sleeper." The object of this exercise is to work for the scene *not* to happen. The "stealing" actor's objective is simply to get the object and get out. If something happens to make the "sleeper" wake, then the "stealer" should attempt to get away with what she is doing. Look at it this way, when you were a teenager still living at home, if you were attempting to sneak back into the house after curfew, did you really want to wake your parents and "have a great scene" or would you rather have gotten to your room without incident? That's the bottom line of this exercise. If the "stealer" is caught, then you do have to speak. However, one of the things I like to do with my students is have them go into a "repetition scene" when or if they have to dialog.

The repetition scene is based on work developed by Sanford Meisner. The following is a brief description.

In the Repetition Exercise actors are only allowed to make observations about their perceptions of the other actor. A simplified example would go something like this:

(Actor 1 wakes to see Actor 2 trying to move silently through the room, but they are obviously in a very agitated state.)

Actor 2:	You're surprised.
Actor 1:	You're projecting.
Actor 2:	I'm projecting. You're miffed.
Actor 1:	I'm miffed.
Actor 2:	You're miffed.
Actor 1:	You're worried.
Actor 2:	I'm worried. You're judging.
Actor 1:	That bothers you.

Actor 2:	That bothers me.
Actor 1:	That bothers you (laughing)
Actor 2:	You find this funny.
Actor 1:	Yes, I find this funny.
Actor 2:	You're self conscious.

The scene should continue until one of the actors gives in to the needs of the other.

This type of scene compels the actor to deal with what's happening from moment to moment. The actor finds that in order to make sense of anything, it is mandatory to listen and pay attention to how the partner is affected by the circumstances. Actors also make some interesting discoveries about how they are affected by circumstances and the partners' responses. Since repetition, though effective, can also be quite tedious, it serves as a wonderful deterrent to student actors who are tempted to "have a scene."

The wonderful thing about "Sleep and Steal" is that it takes all the concepts we work with: simplicity of doing, don't do anything unless something that literally happens makes you do it, public solitude, landscape, trust, guide and voyager, active listening as well as honesty, bringing them all into one doable exercise.

DON'T THINK, JUST DO IT

This is an open scene exercise that works the actors' ability to make quick choices that are both logical and doable. The text of the scene is as follows:

A: There you are.
B: Yeah, here I am.
A: So, what did you do?
B: Just some stuff. You know.
A: Sounds interesting.

B: How about you?

A: Same. Stuff. Just stuff.

B: Is that so? You sure?

A: Yeah.

B: Yeah?

A: Yeah.

B: Oh, well that's good.

A: Yeah.

Each actor should memorize both sets of lines. The purpose for this is so the scene can continue regardless of who needs to start the lines again. If the actors get to the last line and neither has achieved his or her goal, they should continue the scene from the opening line. Either actor can continue the scene. For instance, if actor A says the last line but actor B needs to continue; actor B can continue by using the opening line. The scene would continue with the two actors switching lines but maintaining their character within the circumstance.

The actors will not know what the circumstance is until they are in the performance area. The circumstances for the scene will come from the ensemble. Members of the ensemble should choose clear circumstances that don't require a great deal of explanation. Possible circumstances could be:

1. Lovers meeting after a week long trial separation.
2. Friends suspecting one another of betrayal.
3. A rejection.
4. Siblings making up after a volatile confrontation.
5. Children playing make believe.
6. Parent discovered an object of concern in the room of son/daughter.
7. A blind date.

The actors should be given no more than thirty seconds to prepare. Once the circumstance is given they must make choices that will read with clarity and have a logical conclusion. Based on the actor's work the ensemble should have an idea of the scene's location, the relationship and how the actors arrived at the scene's conclusion.

WORKING WITH THE SCRIPT

"KEEP IT HONEST, KEEP IT SIMPLE"

One of the things which has become a mantra in my work with actors is the idea of keeping the work honest and keeping it simple. As actors we have a tendency toward overpacking. To pack a scene is getting your preparation in order; in film it's called a back-story. Of course you need to answer questions about your characters in order to understand why they do the things they do. You also need to know how they go about dealing with life moment to moment. Just don't overdo it. Actors can analyze a character out of existence if they bog themselves down with too many unnecessary facts. Start out by asking three simple questions, which may help you get a feel for your character:

1. What do people say about me? This question is not limited to other characters in the play. The author says things about your character as well.

2. What do I say about myself? This is not limited to how you describe yourself to others in the play. What do you say about yourself when alone? How do you perceive yourself within the world of the play?

3. Out of everything said about me throughout the play, what's true? Be honest; don't allow character vanity to cloud the answer.

After the above questions are answered, go into more detail. Questions such as the following are a good starting point:

1. Who am I?
2. Where am I?
3. What are the given circumstances?
4. When is it? (time of day, year, etc.)
5. What is around me?
6. How do the things around affect me?
7. Who are the people in my life?
8. How are they affected by the circumstances? Do I care?
9. What is my objective? What needs actually to happen?
10. What obstacles prevent me from obtaining my objective?
11. What actions do I take to obtain my objective?

Remember – don't over analyze; get the information you need in order to live your character's life fully, then stop. If you have the information that's needed, all else should fall gracefully into place as you rehearse and make active discoveries.

NEW YORK STORIES

I have talked endlessly about various exercises which have little or no written text. Here's an exercise that came to me as I looked out my window. I had been working with students at a private college in New York City and was trying to figure out how to get the idea of "dropping in on a character's life" across in a way that would make the most sense. I sat on the edge of the small window in my kitchen, which led out to a postcard-sized balcony, in order to think. As I glanced at a building across the street, I noted movement in one of the windows. A woman was talking to another woman. I shifted my gaze, so that no one would perceive me as a "Peeping Tom," and saw a kid on the phone. I looked down at the sidewalk and saw a couple who looked like they were having an argument. Then I noticed someone, in the building adjacent to mine, watching me, and I slipped back inside. My mind started working over what I had seen, and it dawned on me that I had just looked in on people whose lives had begun long before I saw them and would continue long after I had stopped looking. This is what I had been trying to explain to my students and I had an idea of how to illustrate it.

Take half the scenes that are being worked on and set them in various areas of the studio. Have the actors who are not working at the moment leave the area. Once they have left, have each of the scenes that are in the two or more locations begin simultaneously. The scenes should not be in competition with one another to be heard. The partners in each scene should very simply begin talking to one another and living their lives. Have the other actors quietly re-enter and let them split their attention, viewing one scene, then another, in no order and for as long as the scene holds their attention as individuals. After the first scenes are over, have everyone switch and those actors who were viewing take up new locations according to the needs of their scenes, and the process begins anew. Those who were previously performing are now viewing the other scenes. After everyone has had an opportunity to live in these "windows" and has also sat on the "postcard-sized balcony" and watched these lives unfold, allow them some time to talk through the exercise so that the lesson has the chance to stick.

This exercise brings a couple of things to the forefront. It helps continue the development of the ability to focus on your circumstances regardless of the distractions. It also illustrates the reality that, just because the lights come up doesn't mean that a character's life is just beginning. In the same instance, when the lights fade to black, that character's life doesn't suddenly come to a halt. When preparing keep in mind that in Lorraine Hansberry's play, *A Raisin in the Sun*, Ruth had a life long before she met Walter, Mama and Beneatha, or gave birth to Travis. This life before the play's opening moment sets the tone for who she becomes. Haven't you always wondered what became of that family after they left the little apartment and moved into the all-white neighborhood? If the characters are fully lived in each moment, your audience should wonder what happens after as well.

CONCLUSION

This little book has talked a lot about the need to understand self and how to use that understanding to get in touch with aspects of the character. Through the use of the exercises outlined throughout this book, the author hopes that you, the actor, will get that much closer to understanding. Of course as you make discoveries about yourself, you reveal more of what you are capable of. Oscar Wilde once stated: *I regard the theatre as the greatest of all art forms, the most immediate way in which a human being can share with another the sense of what it is to be a human being.* Each time actors step onto the stage they open up a part of their humanity for public consumption. They reveal aspects of themselves that are not always in view in their personal lives. It's scary to think about, but it's a part of the work. An interesting thing to consider with this idea of sharing what it is truly to be human is that oftentimes the audience is not consciously aware that they are seeing part of who they are deep within.

An idea, which I share with students, is to think of taking what essentially is a one dimensional character on a page and, using these newly revealed aspects of self, coupled with an honest analysis of the play, "breathe life" into it. It isn't something to be afraid of. Embrace the possibilities that lay before you. When you think of revealing your humanity, keep in mind that it doesn't mean the character is really you. The character's humanity is only part of you with imagination and analysis of the script. Break down the character, plot and spine of the script. Find how your character fits into the play and how this affects him or her. Because the character is an incomplete entity without you, look closely at who you are and discover what you have within that will resonate with the character the author created and bring that character to life. Believe in the vast and unexplored landscape before you. Do the work and enjoy the journey.

A FINAL THOUGHT
FROM THE AUTHOR

All of this book's concepts, thoughts, opinions, musings, theories, and so on are based on my personal and professional experiences. I am aware that some of the exercises and theories in this book may not work for every actor. Some will benefit and others may simply use this book as a source for other concepts that work better for them. In the words of poet and songwriter India Arie ...*this is all my opinion, ain't nothin' that I'm sayin's law. This is a true confession, of a life learned lesson, I been sent here to share with y'all.* Like all books on acting, this is in no way a substitute for working with an experienced and credible acting instructor. The key word, of course, is "working." Acting is not a product of magic; it is a product of hard work. No one can wave a glittering wand and have you suddenly become the world's most dynamic and poignant actor. As you wade through and work with all the possible approaches to understanding character through self, you will eventually find what works for *you*. Hopefully, this book and those who have served as an inspiration for its writing have been friendly and useful guides on your ongoing journey.

work space

photo credit: Cynthia Henderson, 2003

Appendix A

GLOSSARY

<u>Acting</u> - Living truthfully in a given circumstance.

<u>Action</u> - The pursuance of a specific goal, in order to further the character's goals or objectives within any moment in the play.

<u>Analysis</u> - The methodical examination of a character or script in order to better understand the character's place in the world of the play. Three useful questions to begin a character analysis are:

What do people say about me?

What do I say about myself?

Of the things said about me, what's true?

<u>As-If</u> - The purpose of the as-if is to assist the actor in personally relating to the character's circumstances (i.e.: *It's as-if ...*). The as-if can

have happened in the actor's life or it can be something which could happen.

Dialog -The verbal exchange between characters, either as an improvisation or text provided by a playwright.

Fourth Wall - An imaginary wall actors erect between themselves and the audience in order to allow for a sense of public solitude.

Given Circumstances - Situation that a character lives in. The circumstances are generally provided by the playwright and/or the director.

Guide - A term used in the *American Book of the Dead* to describe the reader who leads the voyager through the labyrinth. It is used in this book to illustrate the role of actor to audience and to partner.

<u>Labyrinth</u> - A space of uncertainty where the unexpected should always be expected. It is here that guide and voyager meet to begin their journey together.

<u>Landscape Theory</u> - An idea that explores the full potential of human psychological and emotional capabilities. Within that exploration lies the potential of any actor to play any type of character. Everything that is needed to understand the character is already a part of the actor.

<u>Living from one moment to the next</u> - The act of dealing with what is happening in the character's life in the present and then moving into the next moment without hanging on to the previous.

<u>Objective</u> - The primary need of the character in a scene or play. It is also called a through line or goal.

Public Solitude - Living the character's life as-if no one is watching that character.

Safe Space - An agreement between actors working together which allows them to work with full freedom without their process becoming backstage or hallway gossip.

Simplicity of Doing - Release of thoughts which hinder the actor's ability to work on what needs to happen in the circumstances of the scene or play. Simply do what needs to be done without imposing a presupposed emotion or outcome.

Working for the scene not to happen - An idea that allows the actor to give full focus and attention to the objective and scene partner without the need to "have a scene" for its own sake.

SUGGESTED READING

Benedetti, Robert. *The Actor at Work,* Needham Heights, *MA:* Allyn & Bacon, 2001

Bruder, Melissa; Cohn, Lee Michael; Olnek, Madeleine; Pollack, Nathaniel; Previto, Robert; Zigler, Scott. *A Practical Handbook for the Actor,* New York, NY: Vintage, 1986

Cohen, Robert,. *Acting Power,* Palo Alto, CA: Mayfield Publishing Company, 1978

Gold, E.J. *American Book of the Dead,* Nevada City, CA: Gateways/IDHHB, Inc., 2005

Hoff, Benjamin. *The Tao of Pooh,* New York, NY: Penguin Books USA Inc., 1982

Meisner, Sanford; Longwell, Dennis. *Sanford Meisner on Acting,* New York, NY: Vintage, 1987

Needham, Claude. *Just Because Club: Your Personal Metaphysical Fitness Trainer,* Nevada City, CA: Gateways/IDHHB, Inc., 2005

BIBLIOGRAPHY

Arie, India. *Acoustic Soul, Video*. Hollywood, CA: Motown Records, 2001

Bruder, Melissa; Cohn, Lee Michael; Olnek, Madeleine; Pollack, Nathaniel; Previto, Robert; Zigler, Scott. *A Practical Handbook for the Actor*, New York, NY: Vintage, 1986

Gold, E.J. *American Book of the Dead,* Nevada City, CA: Gateways/IDHHB, Inc., 2005

James, William. *The Energies of Men*, New York, NY: Moffat, Yard and Company, 1914

Jung, Carl Gustav. *Man and His Symbols*, Garden City, N.Y.: Doubleday, 1964

Meisner, Sanford; Longwell, Dennis. *Sanford Meisner on Acting*, New York, NY: Vintage, 1987

Modern Language Association. *Acting, Dictionary.com Unabridged (v 1.1)*, New York, NY: Random House, Inc., 2007

Palmer, Edwin H. et al. *The Holy Bible, New International Version: Containing the Old Testament and the New Testament*, Grand Rapids, MI: Zondervan, 1978; Revised 1984

PHOTOGRAPHY CREDITS

Actors appear by their permission in the following photographs (cover photos duplicate others here except for cover photo at top left: Lauren Wightman, Marcin Pawlikiewicz, Chuck Lines, Jonelle Robinson

Title Page: Jonelle Robinson and Michael Haller

Page10 (clockwise from top): Marcin Pawliki-ewicz, Jonelle Robinson, Michael Haller, Lauren Wightman, Matt Musgrove, Abbe Tanenbaum, Chuck Lines, Emily Brazee

Page 18: Emily Brazee

Page 22 ("tangled" from left): Michael Haller, Lauren Wightman,Abbe Tanenbaum, Emily Brazee, Chuck Lines, Jonelle Robinson, Matt Musgrave

Page 24 ("elevate" from left):Jonelle Robinson, Chuck Lines, Matt Musgrove, Abbe Tanenbaum (elevated)

Page 27: Chuck Lines and Matt Musgrove

Page 30: Abbe Tanenbaum and Marcin Paw-likiewicz

Page 33 ("Bliss" 1 and 2): center Lauren Wightman, clockwise from top Abbe Tanenbaum, Marcin Pawlikiewicz, Emily Brazee, Michael Haller, Jonelle Robinson, Matt Musgrove, Chuck Lines

Page 39: Lauren Wightman

Page 43: Emily Brazee and Chuck Lines

Page 53: Matt Musgrove

Page 59 ("energy punches" 1 – 4): Michael Haller, Abbe Tanenbaum, Jonelle Robinson, Chuck Lines

Page 61: Jonelle Robinson

Page 74: Jonelle Robinson and Michael Haller

Page 77: Abbe Tanenbaum and Chuck Lines

All photographs with the exceptions of the following are by Sheryl Sinkow, 2007. Contact Sheryl at *www.sinkowphotography.com.*

Page 103: *Work Space*, by Cynthia Henderson, 2003

Page 113: Photograph of the author, by Justin Baldessare, 2004

ABOUT THE AUTHOR

Photo credit: Justin Baldessare

Cynthia Henderson is a professional actress, a U.S. Fulbright Scholar, and an Associate Professor of acting in the Department of Theatre Arts at Ithaca College in Ithaca, NY. Her professional acting career spans two continents and as many decades. *The Actor's Landscape* was first published in Cameroon, West Africa, by Editions SHERPA. Peace.

NOTES

Dear Reader of *The Actor's Landscape*,

If you are interested in Cynthia Henderson's acting and teaching classes, in workshops that she may be offering, or in further literature related to her method, please contact us at Gateways for current information.

Write:

Gateways Books and Tapes
P.O. Box 370-AL
Nevada City, CA 95959-0370
USA

Phone:

(800) 869-0658 *(in the USA)*
(530) 271-2239
(530) 272-0184 (fax only)

Website:
http://www.gatewaysbooksandtapes.com

email:
info@gatewaysbooksandtapes.com